BEYO...
THE S...

G000125650

Contents

**Jan Burchett
and Sara Vogler**

**Story illustrated by
Martin Aston**

Heinemann

In this story

 Jack

 Aliens

Tricky words

- aliens
- Planet Spot
- spaceship
- spacesuit
- pressed
- space buggy

Introduce these tricky words and help the reader when they come across them later!

Story starter

Jack was just an ordinary boy but he had a magic backpack. When Jack pulled the cord on his backpack – Pop! – something magic popped out. One day, Jack was reading about aliens.

Jack on Planet Spot

"I want to see some aliens," said Jack. "I will put on my backpack and go to Planet Spot."

POP! Out of his backpack came a spaceship. Jack got in.

In the spaceship he saw a spacesuit. Jack put it on.

Jack pressed a green button.
5 ... 4 ... 3 ... 2 ... 1 ... **_Zoom!_**

The spaceship zoomed up into Space.

Jack could see stars and planets.
He could see Planet Spot.

Jack pressed a red button.

BUMP! The spaceship landed on the planet.

Jack jumped out of the spaceship.

ZIP! Into his backpack went the spaceship.

POP! Out of his backpack came a space buggy.
Jack jumped in the space buggy.

8

Jack stopped the space buggy.
He could see rocks and dust.
"There are no aliens here,"
he said.

But there **were** aliens
on Planet Spot!

The aliens came up to Jack.
"Yum! Yum!" they said.

"Aaargh!" said Jack.

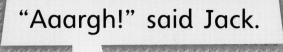 ZIP! Into his backpack went the space buggy.

POP! Out of his backpack came the spaceship.

Jack pressed the green button.

5 ... 4 ... 3 ... 2 ... 1 ... *Zoom!*
The spaceship zoomed up
into Space.

Quiz

HA! HA! HA!

 What did the launch pad say to the rocket?

 "Clear off – you're fired!"

13

Find out about

- The planets in our solar system

Tricky words

- boil
- death
- freeze
- great
- strong
- hurricane
- smallest

Introduce these tricky words and help the reader when they come across them later!

Text starter

There are nine planets that go round our Sun. We live on Planet Earth. You would boil to death on some planets, and freeze to death on other planets. Which planet would you go to?

The Planets

Mercury

Mercury is hot in the day and cold in the night. You would boil to death in the day and freeze to death in the night!

Would you go to Mercury?

Venus

Venus has a long day.
A school day on Venus would be
26 days long!

Would you go to Venus?

Would you like
to go to school

Mars

The rocks on Mars are red. Mars is very cold. You would freeze to death there.

Would you go to Mars?

Jupiter

Jupiter is the biggest planet.
It has a great red spot.
The Great Red Spot is like
a strong hurricane.

Would you go to Jupiter?

Saturn

Saturn has rings.
In the rings are lumps of ice and rocks.

Would you go to Saturn?

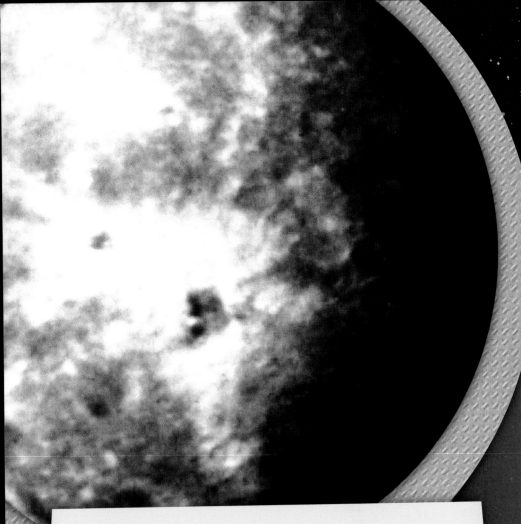

Uranus

Uranus is not as big as Saturn, but it smells bad – like a cowpat!

Would you go to Uranus?

Neptune

Neptune is very windy. The wind is stronger than a hurricane.

Would you go to Neptune?

Pluto

Pluto is the smallest planet.

It is very cold.

Air would freeze on Pluto!

Would you go to Pluto?

Which planet would you go to?

Quiz

Text Detective

- Which is the smallest planet?
- Do you think humans could ever live on another planet?

Word Detective

- **Phonic Focus:** Initial consonant clusters
  Page 23: What are the two phonemes (sounds) at the beginning of 'planet'? Can you blend them?
- Page 17: How many sentences are there on this page?
- Page 18: Find a word that means 'a strong wind'.

Super Speller

Read these words:

would   night   school

Now try to spell them!

HA! HA! HA!

Q What kind of music can you hear in Space?

A A Nep-tune.